Worthing
Then and Now

Tony Wales

Photographs by Bill Young and others.

S.B. Publications

First published in 2003 by S. B. Publications,
19 Grove Road, Seaford, East Sussex BN25 1TP

ISBN 1-85770-281-6

Designed and Typeset by EH Graphics (01273) 515527

Title Page: *Salvation Army leader General Booth visiting Worthing in his newfangled automobile.
Hard to believe, but the Salvation Army was once a cause of considerable unrest in the town,
culminating in riots in 1884. This photo was probably taken in 1907 when such troubles had begun to die down.*

INTRODUCTION

'Worthing - more popular with women from clubs than men from pubs'. Whether this quotation was intended to be complementary or otherwise, I am not sure, but it neatly sums up most published opinions of the town during the past fifty or so years. In other words it is a nice unassuming seaside resort, ideal for families with little to irritate or upset those who look for a quiet stay by the sea.

But indeed it was not always so. In earlier years Worthing provided plenty of excitement - with smugglers, bonfire boys, riots and rowdies. Thankfully most of this is now part of the town's turbulent past, but occasionally it may be instructive to reflect on this side of the town's history, when it lifted its skirts in many irresponsible activities.

Much of this part of Worthing's history has disappeared as the town has adjusted to modern ways. With it has gone the old Town Hall, the early theatre, the fishermen's net shops, the steamers at the end of the pier and the lifeboat house. These are now but memories as the town turns itself into a forward-looking family seaside resort.

I have to confess that I am not a native of Worthing, although I knew it well from my earliest days. More recently I moved to Worthing, living in the town for several years and making many good friends...Eventually the call of my hometown proved too great and I returned to Horsham.

To the many good friends that I made during my happy times in Worthing, I dedicate this little book. I hope that perusing these pictures will revive happy memories for older residents and spark a spirit of enquiry for newer ones.

When this book was originally conceived, the intention was to provide a good selection of 'now' photos taken by Bill Young, who had done similar camera work for the successful book 'Horsham - Then and Now'. Sadly Bill died before he had quite completed his task and I then lost a good friend and colleague. A small number of modern views remained to be captured and these have been splendidly provided by several other photographers.

THEN *THE BEACH* A Directory of 1903 speaks of a long range of smooth sand extending for four miles to the East and nine to the West, sufficiently firm to encourage sea bathing. This turn of the century picture shows a typically busy and varied scene. The beach was often used for many kinds of alfresco entertainments, and once the Worthing Bonfire Boys rolled their tar barrels down South Street to the sands, for their annual fun and games. Even up to the early nineteen-hundreds, Worthing's sedate ladies found reason to complain about male bathers and it was suggested that a screen should be erected to save the ladies' blushes. Fishing has always been carried on from the beaches and a Directory in the early 1900s becomes lyrical in the praise of Worthing herrings. As an insult from their foes, Worthing fishermen were once called 'Pork-bolters', and local fishing folk were taunted with the insult that they had a horror of pigs.

Now A very different picture of modern times, with the beach covered by the incoming tide. However, even on a busy summer's day the sands refuse to look as interesting and animated as they would have done in earlier pictures. But it has to be said that one can still find Worthing fishermen ready to sell you some of their morning's catch.

THEN Worthing's first pier was opened in 1892, having been built at a cost of a little over four thousand pounds. This was a modest edifice, but it included a landing stage at the extreme end from which paddle steamer trips could be enjoyed from 1889, when the pier was lengthened and widened. In 1913 a great storm wrecked the pier and in 1933 fire was responsible for further damage. It was said that on this occasion there was a twenty minute delay in the arrival of the fire brigade and visitors were persuaded to help fight the flames. As with many seaside piers it was said that Worthing's pride had been 'Blown Down, Burnt Out and Blown Up'. In 1939 the pier was closed to the public and did not re-open until ten years later. (Even bathing from the pier, which originally cost threepence, was not permitted.)

Now The kiosks of 1889 have disappeared and the modern theatre greets visitors, who can enter the pier from either side.

THEN *ON THE PIER* In 1913 the Great War was still in the future and visitors on a summer's day enjoyed the pleasures of Worthing's pier. Straw boaters were much in evidence and the long dresses of the ladies did not prevent them from relaxing in the sunshine and sea air. The pencilled message on the other side of this card says that the sender was having a lovely time - paddling and digging - and also that Worthing is a 'very pretty place'.

Now Strolling on the pier on a sunny day may not be as popular as it once was, although Worthing's pier still attracts a fair number of visitors. Steamers appear occasionally, although the threepenny charge for bathing from the pier no longer applies. My own particular memory of the pier is when playing for folk dancing a friendly pigeon decided to make a temporary home in the case containing the band's music.

THEN ***THE LIDO AND BANDSTAND*** Up to the nineteen twenties, Worthing music lovers listened to the band performing in an ornate bandstand typical of the period. This was very much the era of afternoon seaside band concerts for Mum and Dad and Auntie and Uncle, whilst the children not too far away played on the sands. The message on this card mentions that hundreds of youngsters had been making sand castles, which were entered in a competition judged by the Duke of Norfolk from Arundel. Later the bandstand was moved and was replaced by an enclosure with a modest canopy which in 1929 was embellished by a domed roof.

Now   In 1960 the area was modernised and became the Lido Amusement Centre with bandstand, restaurant and other attractions suitable for a rainy day. Less attractive opposite was the very necessary multi-storey car park.

THEN *WEST PARADE* This, the most popular part of the sea front, never fails to attract a large number of visitors on all but the rainiest days. This picture is from around 1919 so the first Great War had barely come to an end. The three smartly turned out soldiers on the left may be home on leave, although the most remarkable part of the picture is the roadway which is almost completely free of traffic apart from the odd horse and cart. The building boom of the thirties is in the future and Worthing is still a quiet, placid seaside resort.

Now If we ignore the cars the modern view is relatively peaceful - although the plethora of traffic signs and street furniture does not help. Many of the large houses fronting the sea have become hotels and boarding houses and Worthing still attracts a large number of summer visitors who enjoy a fairly traditional summer holiday.

THEN *EAST PARADE* This provides a fairly quiet walk between the pier and Splash Point and is always popular on summer Sundays. The picture is from the early 1900s and gives us an interesting view of ladies' fashions of the period. The large wheeled prams were typical of this time and the sedate gardens complement the neatly turned out ladies.

Now Apart from the dress (and the cars) the view has not changed much. Another unchanging feature is the large amount of seaweed that arrives on the beach along this stretch of the coast. Many solutions have been tried, but none seem to have been entirely satisfactory.

THEN *LIFEBOAT HOUSE* Worthing's first Lifeboat House was at the bottom of Heene Lane. This was followed by a purpose-built house close to the pier. The first lifeboat was purchased in 1850 following a disaster in which eleven Worthing fishermen lost their lives. Crowds flocked to the seafront when the lifeboat was launched, sometimes helping by hauling on the ropes fastened to the boat. In 1901 a disaster brought masses of oranges and lemons onto the beach, east of Splash Point. Crowds flocked for this unexpected harvest of the sea and few local families were without fruit for several days afterwards.

Now The Lifeboat House is now a private residence and the occupants can only dream of the exciting times of the past.

(The inset picture shows the Worthing Lifeboat at sea in the last century - although the picture may be a montage dreamed up by a postcard manufacturer.)

THEN *STEYNE GARDENS* A popular stretch of green in the centre of the town often used for fetes and other outdoor events. Steyne Gardens was one of the first open air sites in Worthing to be lit by electric lights, which were fixed to battens in the trees. This picture from c.1906 shows the small bandstand which had been moved from the sea front. It was used for the band in the illuminated concerts which were a popular feature at that time. Other events which attracted crowds were the firework displays.

Now Steyne Gardens without its bandstand, although it is still used regularly for many different kinds of outdoor functions. The trees shelter the grounds from the sea breezes.

Denton Gardens, Worthing.

THEN **DENTON GARDENS** Part of Worthing's wealth of horticultural delights. The Gardens have changed little since they were first laid out on the North side of Beach Walk.

Now Flower lovers still visit this attractive spot so close to the beach and promenade.

THEN *WARNES HOTEL* A picture from the 1920s shows Worthing's most famous hotel as a backdrop to a plane which had ended up on Worthing beach. The hotel started life as a group of separate houses in the 1820s. These were converted by Mr. G.H. Warne to a hotel in 1899. It soon became an important part of Worthing life, being the headquarters of the newly formed Royal Automobile Club. It was visited by King Edward VII and later George V. Later still it became the home of the exiled Emperor Haile Selassie of Abyssinia, when that country was annexed by Italy. Sadly the hotel closed for good in 1985, bringing one of Worthing's most interesting chapters to a close.

Now How the mighty have fallen. The wonderful building, after closing in 1985, was gutted by a fire two years later. Now it exists as a tiny remnant of old Worthing life, sadly ignored by visitors and residents alike. There are plans for flats to be built on the famous site and perhaps the name will survive as a name for the new building.

THEN *THE DOME CINEMA* Worthing's most famous picture house started life as The Kursaal c.1910. It was the brainchild of Carl Adolf Seebold, who was born in 1873 and settled in Worthing in 1904. The original name was unpopular because of its German sound and so The Dome it became. It has seen many changes in its relatively short life, being used as a theatre and cinema in several different forms. Threatened with closure in recent times it has still hung on precariously to life, due mainly to the affection in which the building has always been held. In the front of the picture there appears to be one of Worthing's famous Tramocars. It was in the 1920's that Worthing saw its first tram-like vehicles which were ideal for the flat roads along the sea front. They lasted in several different forms until just before the start of the Second World War.

Now The Dome still survives today, in fact it appears to be heading for a new life as part of a multi-arts centre.

THEN *HOMEFIELD PARK* Originally much larger than at present, this ground was known originally as 'The People's Park' and it included an ornate lake much admired by residents and visitors. Sadly much of the ground (and the lake) were lost when Worthing Hospital was extended.

Now Although less attractive than in its earlier days the park is still used widely, providing a pleasant walk from the popular East Worthing area into Worthing town. It also has the addition of a useful children's play area.

THEN SOUTH STREET looking north from the sea front c.1903. At this time the street was dominated by the Grecian style Town Hall, erected in 1834 with the clock tower above one large room. For its period it was considered a very imposing building, with tall windows showing the activity inside. On the steps 'Old Joe', a familiar crippled figure, offered to clean the shoes of passers by whilst enduring the taunt of local boys. This important site had also been the home of the Town Pump which was removed in the 1850s.

Now Virtually the same spot, but now much changed with different buildings, different street furniture and the old Town Hall missing.

THEN **_THE TOWN HALL_** c.1924, another view but with 1920s traffic. The Town Hall had been built on land donated by Sir Timothy Shelley and was demolished in the 1960s to make way for the Guildbourne Centre. South Street had been a modest lane in the 1700s, with inns on either side kept by men with the interesting names of Hogsflesh and Bacon. This sparked the local rhyme:

Brighton is a pretty place, Worthing is much nicer. If you can't get any other meat, there's still Hogsflesh and Bacon.

Now The Guildbourne Shopping Centre dominates the upper part of South Street. The clock from the old Town Hall may be seen there. Buses tend to take up a lot of the available space in the street itself.

THEN We could not resist one final look at South Street and its Town Hall from 1908. Most of the wheeled traffic is horse drawn apart from the open double-deck omnibus. In 1877 flooding of the town allowed rowing boats to reach almost as far as the Town Hall steps.

Now South Street with one of its most familiar vehicles, the town bus. Also familiar to many residents are the youngster's cycles in the foreground.

THEN *MONTAGUE STREET,* a familiar street corner in c.1909. Montague Street is one of Worthing's most popular shopping areas, now much of it paved. This deserted, but at the same time lively, photo is typical of how shops of this period were unable to restrain their stock from creeping outdoors onto the pavement. No-one ever reported items stolen from outside a shop, although one wonders if this could be so today. The business in the picture could apparently build you a house, decorate it and then sell it.

Now The shop in this modern picture is not worried about tempting its customers inside with a crowded window display. Perhaps modern shoppers are considered much more able to make up their minds before they enter.

THEN *WARWICK STREET* As this commemorative card informs us, Worthing's first Post Office was in Warwick Street, with Mrs Mary Spooner as Postmistress. Later, the handsome building was gutted by fire, but was rebuilt. In its days as a Post Office, it would have been open from 7am in the morning to 10pm at night, with five deliveries on weekdays.

Now As Colonnade House the building still survives in pristine state, but perhaps a little less interesting than in its earlier manifestation.

THEN *ST. PAULS CHURCH,* Chapel Road. It cost a mere £14,000 and was opened in 1812 as a Chapel of Ease to Broadwater Church. Designed by John B. Rebecca, it had to wait until later to be actually designated a Church. Once the handsome frontage was protected by iron railings, with double gates at the front. This view from the early 1900s shows few vehicles apart from a cycle and an interesting invalid carriage propelled by a cycle. The postcard is dated April 4th 1905 and was sent by Florrie, with love to Bessie.

Now St. Paul's Church in modern times, but without its railings and surrounded by a good deal of modern street furniture, which adds little to its charm.

WAR MEMORIAL AND CHAPEL ROAD, WORTHING.

THEN *WORTHING WAR MEMORIAL.* On the corner of Chapel Road and Stoke Abbot Road, this handsome memorial stands 18ft tall and is made of Portland Stone. It honours nearly 700 Worthing men who died in the first Great War (1914 - 1918). The bronze figure represents a British 'Tommy' from the 'War to end wars'. The ladies in the photo are wearing typical outfits and hats of the 1920s.

Now Little changed apart from the traffic and the fact that the names of the soldiers who died in the Second World War have been added to the Memorial.

THEN ***CHAPEL ROAD*** c. 1912. Originally a row of private houses, which was later on to become one of Worthing's most important business roads, with many high class shops. Once there were two large drapers who were great rivals. One had 'Shilling Days' when hats, dresses and ladies underwear were offered at this low figure. Business hours were 8am to 8pm Mondays to Thursdays, with Fridays until 9pm and Saturdays until 10pm. Pity the poor shop assistants. But the shoppers liked it and the town would be full of people on these late nights, with Mr Vine offering a joint for ninepence and a pudding for threepence.

Now No longer these long hours, but still important as a shopping area, with pedestrians dodging the parked cars. What a pity the banners have disappeared.

THEN ***WORTHING HOSPITAL.*** This is in Lyndhurst Road, well placed in the centre of town to serve its residents. Originally it was known as 'Worthing Infirmary and Dispensary' and was built in 1881 at the surprisingly modest cost of something between three and four thousand pounds. The building boasted sixteen beds and eight children's cots. A separate children's ward was added in 1889 at a cost of £600. Well used and well loved, it continued to offer health care for residents of the Worthing area well into the late twentieth century, with additional buildings being added as required.

Now In time to feature in our 'Then and Now' compilation, the new Worthing Hospital replaced the old at the beginning of the new century. Sparkling new wards, shops and cafes, what seem to be miles of corridors and of course masses of modern equipment, are now available to residents of Worthing and the surrounding area.

THEN *BROADWATER BRIDGE* c.1906. A tranquil countrified scene of the railway bridge leading out of Worthing town to nearby Broadwater, with the South Downs faintly showing in the background. Close by was The Bridge Pharmacy run by Mr Frost, who besides normal business would pull teeth without an appointment.

The same spot although almost unrecognisable, apart from the trees on either side. Much of the rest of the picture is taken up by new building.

THEN *WORTHING RAILWAY STATION.* The railway came to Worthing in 1845, although the present station was built in 1868 and rebuilt in 1911. This picture shows part of the station after electrification.

 Now The same platform, very little changed, apart from a few extra weeds on the lineside.

THEN *ST. GEORGE'S CHURCH* c.1915. The church was built in 1868 to serve a newly formed parish. Writing in 1960 (in his book Alexandra Terrace) Mr A. Longley described the setting of the church at that time: 'The church stood practically on its own. To the West one saw isolated houses and to the East a vista of meadowland.' But industry was coming to the parish - brickmakers at work in Ham and Brougham Roads - and the glasshouses arrived.

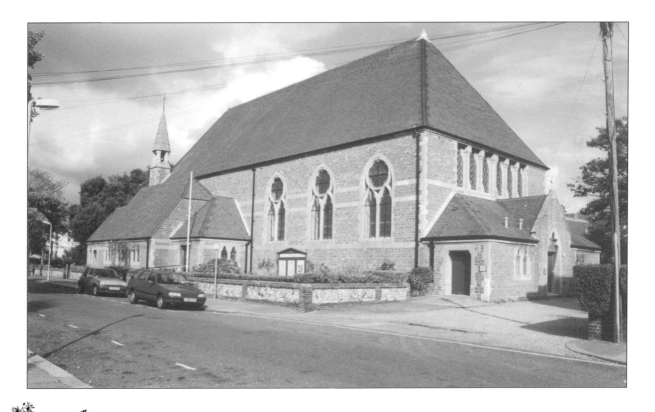

Now The building little changed, with even its attractive brick wall still intact. The main difference is the addition of several cars and white parking lines on the road.

THEN *HEENE ROAD.* Once Heene was considered a separate entity to Worthing. From the 1890s it developed rapidly, often being known as West Worthing - even with its own railway station.

Now Heene has lost its countrified look and is now very much a part of Worthing town, although residents still like to feel that they live in a very special area.

THEN *MANOR ROAD, HEENE.* The old parish and manor of Heene has its own separate history. The present church of St. Botolphs dates from 1873 although the original church had a history going back to medieval times. Heene was mentioned in the Domesday Book when Worthing was but an unimportant hamlet.

 Now Manor Road is still tree lined, emphasising the quiet nature of much of Heene.

THEN *HIGHDOWN.* The Miller's Tomb seen in the early 1900s. Miller Oliver was a local celebrity and eccentric. Obsessed with death, he had his coffin on wheels under his bed. He built his own tomb when he was 84 and this still stands although his mill was demolished in 1826. Children used to believe that the Latin inscription on the tomb said that anyone running round it, twelve times at midnight, would make either the miller or the devil appear. His funeral was attended by 2,000 maidens dressed in white (or so it was said). One of the young ladies read a sermon written by Oliver. Many stories surround this site, including one that says the Miller was buried upside down. He was also reputed to be a smuggler and the path from Highdown is sometimes referred to as Smugglers Walk.

Now The Miller's tomb may still be seen today, although it has been rebuilt in more recent times. Even today stories are still told of the Miller's ghostly appearances. Many Saxon artefacts have been found in this area, so this is undoubtedly an important ancient burial ground.

THEN *FERRING.* This is one of the many attractive coastal villages that have become almost part of big brother Worthing in modern times. Close by is the famed Highdown Hill, with its many tales and legends, attracting masses of visitors during the summer months. However, Ferring once had its own attractions. In spring there was Garland Day, still observed by local children up to the 19th century. One year a youngster arrived at school 'Noisy and almost intoxicated, having spent his Garland Money on strong drink'.

Now In the modern picture the car spoils what would otherwise be a tranquil country scene. Even the large house in the first picture has now been obscured by greenery.

THEN *BROADWATER CHURCH.* The church dates from the late 12th Century. For many years it was the most important church in Worthing, as the Mother Church. (Until 1826 it had a small spire.) Stories connect the church with smugglers and it was said that the verger often helped them by hoisting a flag on the church tower. There are also stories of a secret tunnel leading to the church. Broadwater cemetery is a mile away, comprising ten acres and two chapels. Here are buried two famous writers - Richard Jefferies and W.H. Hudson.

Now Even as recently as the 1920s a thatched barn stood near the church, but now it is part of an extremely busy and noisy street corner.

THEN *BROADWATER.* This tranquil scene from early 1900s bears little resemblance to the busy Broadwater of today. Once it was more important than Worthing - an 1835 book speaks of the latter as a hamlet of Broadwater.

Now A typical Broadwater street scene in recent times, with cars the dominant features. However, Broadwater still has its history. A local tale recalls the Midsummer Oak - a large tree that stood near the Common. At midnight each year a group of skeletons were said to emerge from the roots and dance round the tree until cockcrow. (The story was printed in 1868, although the account is still recalled by some older residents.)

THEN *BROADWATER ROAD.* This is the upper part of the main road through Broadwater, showing the popular Cricketers Pub. Not far away lies Broadwater Manor, which later became a school. The school building is of many different periods, with flint rubble walls at its heart and lovely cream bricks said to have been manufactured with materials from Worthing seashore. The doorways are particularly wide and a pupil suggested to me that these were made in this fashion for the convenience of ladies wearing crinoline-hooped skirts. Local folklore says a tunnel ran from the Manor to the church and I was shown a spot where this may have existed.

 Now The Pub survives although much of the surrounding buildings have given way to shops.

Offington Corner.

THEN *OFFINGTON CORNER.* The Gaisford family were the last residents of Offington Hill, which was demolished several years ago. Since the 1930s the area has been developed for residential use and what was once a popular country scene for picture postcards has now become a busy part of Broadwater.

Now This is close to what is left of Broadwater Green. Originally this was much larger, with fairs being held there and close by a large pond. There was a huge chestnut tree, from which wood was used to make tables for the saloon bar of the nearby Cricketers Inn.

THEN ***GORING CROSS ROADS.*** Goring in the early 19th century was a little different to that of today. Then Squire Stanhope drove about the village in a horse and trap, with his silver hair tied back with a ribbon. At Christmas time the Goring Wassailers sang 'Send out your eldest daughter, if you will be so kind. Send out your eldest daughter with strong beer and some wine'. The famed nature writer Richard Jefferies lived his final years in Goring, dying there in 1887.

Now Pity the poor modern photographer who had to decide exactly where the original crossroads fitted in with the present road system. A quiet country lane has become a busy housing estate, with thatch replaced by modern building materials. Happily a few trees still survive.

THEN *THOMAS a' BECKET CORNER, TARRING.* A group of mock Tudor buildings, with the familiar Tarring name recalling the saint who tends to make an appearance all over Tarring. Although there is no evidence that the Archbishop ever lived in the village, no true Tarring resident would ever agree that the saint was not closely connected with the place during his lifetime. Saint Thomas was born in London in 1117, studied in Paris and became a leading figure in the English church. He was murdered, due it was said to a tragic misunderstanding, in his own cathedral on December 29th 1170.

Now Now St Thomas is remembered in Tarring by several local street names and buildings, proving that tradition is stronger than dry-as-dust history tomes.

THEN *PARSONAGE ROW, TARRING.* The timber framed buildings of Tarring suffered in 1895 when the Southern end of Parsonage Row was demolished. The rest was saved by the Sussex Archaeological Society and for some years one of the cottages was used as a Museum of Sussex Folklore. The inn sign of the George and Dragon was welded into an upright position in 1927, as the local Southdown double-deck buses persisted in hitting it as they went past.

Now The old gentleman with his top hat has long passed into history and modern cars cope with the old world charm of this lovely Sussex street.

THEN ***WEST TARRING CHURCH.*** **This is how the church looked in 1875. (By 1983 a writer noted that the field had 'now become a bowling green'.) The church was built in the late 13th century, with the chancel and tower added in the 15th. Two items of folklore have long been attached to the church. One is that the spire has a slight twist, which was because of the suicide of the architect who designed it. The other belief is that the church is one of the few unofficial buildings allowed to fly the white ensign.**

 Now West Tarring Church as it looks today. Full of the beauty of the ages, with a lovely tranquil feel to its setting.

THE ANCIENT
FIG GARDENS
TEAS
PROVIDED

THEN *TARRING FIG TREES.* A view from c.1900 of the fig gardens in South Street. The trees were said to date from 1745 and legend insists that they were planted originally by St. Thomas a' Becket. The fig trees are cited as evidence of the mildness of the climate. The fig gardens were owned for some years by Mr and Mrs Wadey, who ran them as a tourist attraction. (Edward Lear stayed here, sketching the trees.) Until the Second World War Miss Humphries ran the tea garden.

Now In 1988 a large part of the fig gardens disappeared during modern building. Now only a few gardens have fig trees, although occasionally these are open to the public.

THEN *ARCHBISHOP'S PALACE, TARRING.* Certainly Becket owned land in Tarring, although whether this was actually his palace we are not sure. The building is said to date from 1230 and was used as the local school from 1872. In 1985 the children were moved to a new Thomas a' Becket school, so his name lives on.

 Now The bishop's palace is still an important building and is used as a local hall.

THEN *LANCING BEACH.* A fine stretch of clean sands, much appreciated by local fishermen. The area has a history of smuggling and much tea and brandy must have passed this way in the past. Part of the beach was known as 'Lancing Shops', with a track leading to the historic Sussex Pad Inn where the smugglers had their headquarters.

Now Lancing Beach in more modern times. One of the fishermen's boats is being blessed in an annual ceremony.

THEN *LANCING STATION.* The station has been little changed since it was built in the 19th century and this picture shows it on a typical day in the 1920s. In 1930 the normal life of this country station was disturbed when a Schools Class Locomotive was christened 'Lancing College' at a naming ceremony. Much of the local railway life was centred around the Lancing Carriage Works which had been opened on a 66-acre site.

Now Lancing Station today, waiting for the daily commuters to Worthing or Brighton.

THEN *LANCING LEVEL CROSSING* c. 1906. The railway came to Lancing in 1845. When the carriage works moved from Brighton it provided a new source of local employment, vying with the nurseries and market gardens who had previously been the main providers of jobs in the area.

Now The rail crossing today. The signal box had a strange item of folklore attached to it, as it was said that it was demolished by local strong man Alfred Blaker when he accidentally leant on it.

THEN *OLD COTTAGE, NORTH LANCING.* This is at the junction of Manor Road and Mill Road and is said to be the oldest house in Lancing (parts may be as early as the 13th century). Many notables are reputed to have stayed here, including Charles II on his way to Shoreham. There are many good stories attached to the house, including one that says the internal timbers were taken from galleons wrecked on the beach. In the 1950s a Priest's Hole from Reformation days was discovered in the attic.

 Today the cottage is still visited and admired by many visitors to Lancing who marvel at its beautiful simplicity.

THEN *SALVINGTON POST MILL.* This is on the top of the hill at High Salvington and is Worthing's last surviving windmill. It was last worked as a mill on a daily basis around 1914. In the 1930s it was used as a tearoom and it is shown in this guise on many picture postcards. Said to be the last surviving 'post and socket' mill in Sussex, so well balanced that the miller's daughter could turn it single-handed. It has the rare distinction of being the first windmill to have been insured against fire.

Now   Between the wars it fell into disrepair, until it was faithfully restored by volunteers in recent times. Today it is owned by a Trust, with open days and a flourishing association ' The Friends of Salvington Mill'. A new barn has been built close to the mill and open days are attended by many visitors from a wide area.

THEN *SOMPTING CHURCH.* As it appeared in the early 1900s. The church is the great treasure of the village, in fact of Sussex as a whole. It is famed for its Saxon tower with its Rhenish Helm, a most unusual feature. Mentioned in the Domesday Book, the church can claim a history of over 900 years. Many Sussex folk who have lived overseas for many years remember this church as something unique in local history and paintings and picture postcards of the church turn up in all kinds of unexpected places.

Now Thankfully the building is little changed in its rural setting. Sompting village has little claim to fame otherwise, unless one includes the imaginary Treacle Mines. Similar mines exist over the whole of the country and here they are attached to anyone who is considered to be especially lazy. The particular authority on the mines has always been Jimmy Smuggles, a famous (although completely imaginary) local character.

THEN *FINDON.* A familiar part of the original village of Findon, not to be confused with the more modern Findon Valley. Since, it is said, the thirteenth century Nepcote Green at Findon has been associated with an annual sheep fair. (The original date of the fair - September 14th - was always considered locally to be the right date to start indoor fires.) Even within living memory vast numbers of sheep were driven through the Downland roads to the fair each year looking, as one observer said, like 'Fluffy white clouds'. The sheep may be gone but the fair still continues each year.

Now Findon, with its memories of fairs and shepherds, still survives. You may still find a resident who can answer the local riddle 'Why are all the blacksmiths in Findon coloured men?' (The answer is that at one time there were three local smiths - a Mr Brown, a Mr White and a Mr Green.)

52856

THEN *THE DOWNS (AND CHANCTONBURY RING).* A classic view of the Downs, so beloved of most Worthing residents, and said to be one of the best views in England. From Chanctonbury Ring it is said that you can see nearly the whole of Sussex. The famous clump of trees planted by Charles Goring of Wiston in 1760 was all but destroyed in the storm of 1987. Until then a local riddle was to ask someone to provide an estimate of the number of trees on the crown.

Now A modern picture of the Ring from the book 'West Sussex Walks'. Although the famous trees were decimated in 1987 the folklore surrounding this most famous part of Sussex still remains. For instance, if you run seven times around the Ring the Devil will appear and provide you with a bowl of soup. (Your own version of this tale may be different, as there are many variants.)

ACKNOWLEDGEMENTS

For photography:
Bill Young
Joy Street (for her valuable assistance to Bill Young)
David Brook
Steve Benz
and others.

For use of old photographs and other information:
Cecil Cramp
John Cannon
Chris Hare

For the very valuable assistance in completing the book, I am indebted to my daughter Sue Wales, for her knowledge and patience.

BIBLIOGRAPHY

Davies, Roger: *Tarring.* 1990.
Hare, Chris: *Historic Worthing. 1991. Worthing.* 1997.
Kelly's *Directory of Sussex.* 1903.
Longley, A: *Alexandra Terrace.* 1960.
Migeod, F.W.H: *Worthing.* 1938.
Swinfen, Warden and Arscott, David: *Hidden Sussex - The Towns.* 1990.
Watts, Jack: *Old Worthing as I remember it.* 1975.
White, Dr. Sally: *Around Worthing.* 1991.
Worthing and District Blue Book. 1934-5.
Plus various town guides and newspapers.